ANIMAL FAMILIES

Elephants

angus

This edition published in 2004
by Angus Books Ltd
12 Ravensbury Terrace
London SW18 4RL

ISBN 1-904594-59-X

FOR BROWN PARTWORKS LIMITED

Author: Daniel Gilpin
Consultant: Dr. Adrian Seymour
Project editor: Tim Harris
Managing editor: Anne O'Daly
Picture research: Adrian Bentley
Index: Margaret Mitchell

PICTURE CREDITS

Artworks: AntBits Illustration

BBC Natural History Unit: (Simon King) 21. *Bruce Coleman Collection*: (Alain Compost) 26; (HPH Photography) 10, 27; (J. P. Zwaenepoel) 22; (Jen & Des Bartlett) 4; (Mary Plage) 11 below. *Corbis*: (Kevin Schafer) 28. *NHPA*: (Andy Rouse) 23; (Daryl Balfour) contents page, 5 above, 8, 19; (John Shaw) 15 above, 17 below; (Kevin Schafer) 9; (Martin Harvey) title page, 6, 12, 14–15, 15 below, 20–21, 29; (Nigel J. Dennis) 7; (T. Kitchin & V. Hurst) 17 above. *Papilio*: (Mike Buxton) 11 above; (Robert Gill) 16. *Still Pictures*: (M. & C. Denis-Huot) 13; (Mark Carwardine) 24; (Mathieu Laboureur) front cover, 18; (Roland Seitre) 5 below.

Series created by Brown Partworks Limited.
Designed by Wilson Design Associates

Production by Omnipress,
Eastbourne, UK
Printed and bound in Dubai

Contents

Introduction

Elephants are fascinating creatures. They are the biggest land-living animals on the planet and among the most unusual ones too. Their trunks, tusks, and giant ears give them a unique appearance, and their power and strength are unequaled on land.

As well as being powerful, elephants are intelligent. They have large brains that grow through youth, giving them a great capacity to learn. In fact, they display some behaviours only seen in a few other animals.

Elephants are mammals, like we are. They make caring mothers, showing great tenderness to their young.

There are two species (types) of elephants. One species lives in Africa; the other lives in Asia.

▼ *The African elephant is the largest land animal. Its long trunk and large ears make it unmistakable.*

▲ *An African elephant pauses by a waterhole.*

Tool use

Elephants are among the few creatures known to use tools. Wild elephants have been seen using twigs and branches to brush away flies or scratch themselves. Elephants are the only animals apart from monkeys and other primates that can throw things. Using their trunk like an arm, they sometimes pick up objects and hurl them at other animals or people.

Above all, elephants are social animals. They all spend at least part of their lives in groups. Some elephants never leave the groups they were born into.

In this book you will learn all about how elephants live together. Later on you will find out more about just what makes them such special animals.

The elephant's trunk

The elephant's trunk is an amazing piece of natural engineering. Most people think that an elephant's trunk is its nose, but it is actually a combination of its nose and its upper lip. It contains more than 100,000 different muscle units, making it very flexible and easy to maneuver. Elephants use their trunks to pick up food, suck up water, caress one another, fight, and of course, smell. Elephants also use their trunks to make a noise, called trumpeting.

▲ *The underside of an elephant's muscular trunk.*

Elephant society

Most elephants live in groups called herds. The basic elephant herd is an extended family of female elephants and their young. Adult male, or bull, elephants normally live alone or in temporary herds of their own. They only join the permanent female herds when they are looking for a mate.

The females in the basic elephant herd are always related. They spend their whole lives together, and the bonds between them are strong. They help each other raise and protect the young, they travel together, and they feed as a group. Herd members rarely move more than about 50 yards (15m) apart.

African elephant herds range from two to about 24 animals. Sometimes herds of related female elephants join to form groups of 50 or so members, called clans. Asian elephants have smaller herds of usually ten or fewer animals. If herds get too big, they split in two. These herds keep in contact and often meet, with a lot of excitement and friendly trumpeting noises.

Elephant herds do not have actual territories, but each does have certain areas where it can often be found. These areas may be shared with other herds.

▼ *A herd of female elephants with their calves. Most of the females in a herd are related, and they help each other take care of the young.*

Occasionally, a number of African elephant herds will gather to form a superherd. These giant herds can have more than 500 individuals in them and contain both males and females. Superherds form in areas where there is lots of food.

The leader of the herd is the matriarch. She is the oldest and largest female, and she makes decisions that affect the others. The matriarch leads the herd to find new feeding grounds. When she stops to feed, the rest of the herd stops with her.

▲ *A lone bull elephant in a national park in Namibia, Africa.*

Washing off and dusting down

Elephants seem to enjoy bathing more than anything else. When they reach a river or deep watering hole, they often wade right in before even taking a drink. Bathing cleans the skin and cools down the elephants. But it is also a social activity, giving adults a chance to relax and youngsters an excuse to play.

Getting the message across

Elephants are great communicators. With their trunks and huge ears they have very good senses of smell and hearing, and they use both of them to keep in touch.

◄ *Communication is an important part of elephant society. It helps animals stay together, warn of danger, and express feelings such as anger and fear.*

Elephants can communicate over very long distances. They can send messages across several miles (kilometers) using infrasound (see the box). They also use infrasound as well as normal sound to communicate at closer range.

When they can see each other, elephants use body language, touch, and smell much more. The ears are used like flags. They are spread out to show aggression or dominance and flattened back against the head to indicate submission or fear.

The trunk is also used for communication. When two elephants meet after being apart, one puts its trunk into the other's

► *These male African elephants are greeting each other by touching their trunks.*

Rumbles in the jungle

Most people know that elephants make trumpeting noises. But not long ago it was discovered that they make many more sounds as well. Using special equipment, scientists have found that elephants use very low-pitched sound, or infrasound, to communicate with each other. Infrasound is too low-pitched for humans to hear ("infra" means below). But for a large animal like an elephant the sound is easy to pick up. Elephants use infrasound to communicate over long distances. Unlike ordinary sound, infrasound does not get broken up by trees and bushes. Infrasound is also produced by thunderstorms. Scientists think that this might explain why elephants are able to sense approaching rain long before humans can.

mouth in a greeting ceremony. Swinging the trunk forward is a threat. Mothers reassure their infants by touching them with their trunks.

Elephants have a very fine-tuned sense of smell. They raise their trunks and sniff the air to get information about their surroundings. They can recognize different members of the herd by their odour, and they can smell elephants from outside the herd too. They may even be able to tell when another elephant is becoming excited or angry by changes in its smell.

Food and feeding

Elephants are the largest land animals on Earth. A fully grown bull African elephant can weigh up to 8 tons (7.3 tonnes)—the weight of more than 100 people. Being this big has its advantages, but it makes finding enough food each day a full-time job.

An adult male elephant eats up to 350 pounds (159kg) of plant matter every day. He can spend 18 hours a day looking for it. To make life easier, elephants feed on a wide range of plant species. They have been found to eat between 100 and 500 different kinds of plants, depending on where they live.

The reason why elephants can eat so many different plants is that they can feed at many different levels. Using its trunk, an elephant can tear grass from the ground or reach up to strip leaves from the high branches of trees. It can also pick up fallen fruit or rip away tree bark that it has loosened with its tusks.

▲ *An African elephant uses its trunk like an arm to pluck leaves from the branches of a tree.*

Drinking

Elephants drink a lot of water. An adult African elephant can drink up to 50 gallons (190 l) a day. An elephant drinks by using its trunk to suck up water and then squirts the water into its mouth.

Elephant herds usually travel to water at least once a day but can go without it for more than two weeks. They prefer some watering holes to others, choosing those with high amounts of salt and other minerals in the water.

▲ *Elephants use their trunks to drink. An elephant's trunk can hold up to 10 pints (5.7 l) of water.*

▼ *This Asian elephant is feasting on newly grown grass soon after the rains.*

Once it has grasped the food with its trunk, an elephant passes the food up to its mouth. There, four huge molar teeth (two in each jaw) crush and grind the food before the animal swallows. Food takes between 22 and 46 hours to pass through the body. What comes out is still 60 percent undigested. Elephant dung provides food for many smaller animals as well as being excellent fertilizer for the soil of the plains and forests where elephants live.

Elephants need so much food that they spend nearly every waking hour feeding. The herd munches through much of the day and almost all of the night as well. True sleep is just two or three hours around noon (the hottest time of the day) or just after midnight.

The mating game

When they are about 10 or 11 years old, female elephants first become able to mate. When she is able to mate, a female elephant is said to be "in estrus." Estrus does not last all year round but just for two to six days. If a female elephant does not mate during this time, she will come into estrus again about 16 weeks later.

Females in estrus attract nearby males to mate with them. When she starts to come into estrus, a female elephant often walks in an unusual way, with her head held high and looking back over her shoulders.

This is called an estrus walk, and it may help draw males to her. Females in estrus also make special sounds. Some of these sounds can be heard by humans; others are too low. These sounds may help attract roaming males.

▼ *African elephants choosing a mate. They stroke each other with their trunks as part of their courtship.*

Once she has attracted a bull, the female elephant usually urinates to let him test her estrus state by smell. If she has started her estrus properly, the male responds in an excited way. At this point female African elephants walk quickly away, making the bulls chase them.

Female elephants are quicker than males, so, if she is not impressed by her partner, she can easily get away from him. If she does like him, she will let him catch up with her, and the pair will mate. The largest bull elephants are most popular with females, and bulls in must always win the right to mate over those not in must.

Asian elephants have a slightly different mating behaviour from African elephants. Asian elephants stand face to face and twine their trunks together before mating.

An elephant pregnancy is more than twice as long as a human pregnancy. Once a female elephant has mated, she carries her unborn baby growing inside her for more than 22 months.

▲ A bull elephant in must dribbles oily liquid from glands just behind his eyes. This liquid has a strong, musky smell, which the bull spreads by flapping his ears. The timing of must varies between different bull elephants, so some are in must while others are not.

Must

About once every year adult bull elephants go through a change in their behaviour known as must. Must is caused by increased levels of the male hormone, testosterone. Bulls in must are much more aggressive than usual, and other bulls usually keep away from them. But sometimes two must bulls meet. When this happens, they fight violently. Such fights can result in severe injury or even death.

Babies and youngsters

Baby elephants can walk within an hour, but they are very shaky on their feet for the first few days. The mother stays close to her offspring for the whole of the first year. She feeds the young elephant on her milk, protects it from enemies, and uses her body to shade it in the heat of the day.

Growing up

Baby elephants start off big and then just get bigger. A newborn African elephant weighs about 265 pounds (120kg). By the time it is six years old, it tips the scales at a ton (0.9 tonnes). Elephants grow all their lives. They slow after they turn 15, but bulls have an extra spurt between 20 and 30, which is when they become much bigger than females.

The other females in the herd all help with bringing up baby. If the mother is separated from her calf for any reason, one of the other females rushes to its side to comfort it. These elephant "aunts" will even let a youngster comfort-suckle.

When they are not feeding or travelling with the herd, baby elephants spend a lot of time playing. They explore new objects, sometimes picking them up and throwing them or rolling them along the ground. They charge playfully at smaller animals, birds, and bushes, and they jostle with each other.

Young males in particular spend a lot of time wrestling and chasing one another around.

14

► *Play teaches baby elephants skills, such as how to use their trunks. It also lets young males test their strength against others.*

▼ *African elephant calves rely on their mother's milk until they are two years old.*

As they get older, they find new and unfamiliar partners for these games. By the time they are six or seven years old, they have started leaving the herd for short periods. They search for different families to find males of a similar age to spar with.

Young females gradually grow out of play and begin to take more responsibility within the herd. At five or six years old they start to help with looking after the smallest babies. They keep an eye on them while the mother is busy and sometimes guard them while they sleep.

▼ *Mother elephants use their trunks to guide and reassure their young calves.*

Males

Young male elephants start to become adults at about 12 years old. Their play gets more aggressive, and they spend more and more time away from the herd looking for other young males to spar with. Eventually, at about 15 or 16 years old, male elephants leave the herd they grew up in for good.

Some go of their own accord; others take a little persuading. As young males become more aggressive, the older females start to lose patience with them. Eventually, the females drive the youngsters away from the herd.

Once they have left, male elephants behave in different ways. Some become solitary wanderers, while others form temporary all-male groups. A few join a different family herd. They stay with it for up to a year before becoming independent.

While they are in their late teens and early twenties, bull elephants keep the herding instinct. They often join large groups of females for short periods or travel with other bulls. All-male herds are good places for the younger bulls to test their strength and get to know their future rivals.

▼ *Bull elephants spend months at a time in "retirement areas." They are places where bulls live when they are not looking for a mate.*

Fully grown bulls spend a lot of time wandering from herd to herd, particularly when they are in must, looking for females that are ready to mate. As bull elephants get older, they spend more time on their own. The oldest bulls are almost always solitary. Most stay near swamps where there is plenty of water and vegetation soft enough to chew with their worn-out teeth.

Aggressive behaviour

Male elephants fight from an early age. Even as babies they find youngsters of a similar size to tussle with. As they get older, their fighting becomes more serious. Bulls joining an all-male group for the first time wrestle with the others to establish their rank. Must bulls battling for estrus females may even fight to the death. Some males test their strength in other ways. Tree-felling is a particular favourite. With the right technique a bull elephant can topple a tree as much as 5 ft (1.5m) high.

▲ A young African bull destroys a tree.

▼ Two bulls clash in a head-to-head fight. A battle between bulls in must can last up to six hours!

Females

Female elephants spend their whole lives in the family groups they were born into. When they start to become adults, they play less and spend more time helping look after the younger members of the herd. Eventually, they become old enough to mate and attract the attention of adult males.

Most female elephants first mate when they are 10 or 11 years old. The bonding between females in the elephant herd is strong. Most herds are extended family groups, and all the females in them are closely related. Because they are all either mothers, daughters, sisters, or cousins of one another, they work together to look after the young. When a mother is

▼ A group of females of different ages visits a waterhole. All will be related to each other.

Birth

Female elephants have their first baby when they are 12 or 13. Some females prefer to give birth surrounded by the rest of the herd. Others leave for a short while to have the baby on their own. Elephants give birth standing up, and the baby has quite a drop before it hits the ground. The mother turns around to check the little infant as soon as it is born, examining it with her trunk and gently nudging it with one of her front feet. If she has given birth surrounded by the herd, other females help her remove the membrane covering the baby and may help getting it up on its feet.

feeding, a younger female watches over her baby to make sure it does not get into difficulties. And when faced by a predator, the whole herd forms a wall of trunks and legs to shield the infants. It must be a menacing sight for a would-be attacker.

Female elephants never grow as big as the adult males, nor do they grow such long tusks. Female Asian elephants hardly have tusks at all.

▼ *The matriarch leads the herd. When she reaches 50 to 60 years old, she is replaced by the next-oldest female.*

Elephants and death

Elephants are among the longest-lived of all animals. Wild African elephants can easily reach 60 years old, and wild Asian elephants are thought to live beyond 70. The oldest-known tame Asian elephant lived to be 78.

Because of their size adult elephants have very few predators. Diseases kill some elephants when they are still young, but many live to old age. The main natural killer of elephants is starvation. Every elephant gets six sets of bricklike molar teeth in its lifetime. Once the sixth set has worn out, the elephant can no longer feed, and it starves to death.

▼ *An African elephant touches the body of a companion who has died of natural causes.*

Apart from starvation the main killer of elephants is humans. Poaching their tusks for ivory and culling to prevent overpopulation means that many African elephants never get to reach a natural death. Asian elephants are not hunted in the same way, and most of them live to old age.

Elephants show some behaviour that suggests they have some understanding of death. Whenever elephants come across the remains of others of their kind, they become very excited. They explore the bones with their trunks. They even pick some bones up and throw them or roll them around with their feet.

◄ *A young Asian elephant sniffs the bones of a dead elephant.*

Exploding the myth

For centuries people have told stories about elephant graveyards. They are supposed to be secret places where elephants go to die. The tales are partly based on fact. There are places in Africa and Asia where large numbers of elephant skeletons have been found gathered together. Myths have grown up about these places. They suggest the elephants are drawn there by mysterious forces. But scientists think that there is a simpler explanation. They point out that sick and dying elephants usually head to areas where there is plenty of food and water, such as swamps and waterholes. The elephants die in these places, and their bones collect over the years.

Shape and size

With its long trunk, enormous ears, and tusks an elephant looks like nothing else on Earth. Each of these strange appendages has its purpose. They help the elephant survive.

Apart from the trunk, an elephant's ears are its most obvious feature. But why are they so big? The main reason is that they help elephants cool down. Each ear is filled with hundreds of blood vessels. As the blood flows through the vessels in the ear, heat escapes through the skin into the surrounding air. When the weather is really hot, elephants flap their ears, which helps them lose heat even more quickly.

The tusks are actually giant incisor teeth. Elephants use their tusks to pull up roots, tear the bark off trees, and dig out waterholes. They also use their tusks as weapons. Tusks are made from a creamy-white substance called ivory. In the past ivory was used to make ornaments and jewelry. Many elephants were killed for their ivory tusks.

Elephants from different areas have different shapes and sizes. An average adult bull African savanna (or bush) elephant weighs up to 7 tons (6.4 tonnes) and stands 12 ft (3.6m) tall. The tallest African elephants live on the Skeleton Coast of Namibia in southwest Africa. The biggest Asian elephants live on the island of Sri Lanka. They weigh up to 5 tons (4.5 tonnes) and measure 11.5 ft (3.5m) at their shoulder.

The smallest elephants are the forest elephants of central and west Africa. They have long, straight tusks and oval ears.

▼ *It is easy to tell an Asian elephant, such as this one, from its African cousin. Asian elephants have smaller ears and a domed head. Their bodies tend to be smaller and chunkier, too.*

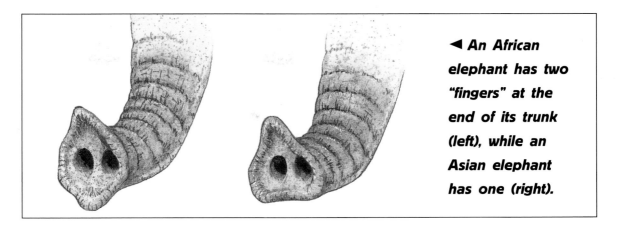

▼ *An African savanna elephant's ears make up one-seventh of its body surface.*

◄ *An African elephant has two "fingers" at the end of its trunk (left), while an Asian elephant has one (right).*

Elephant evolution

Elephants have existed on Earth for around 50 million years. The earliest elephant looked nothing like an elephant. It was called *Moenitherium*. It was about the size of a pig and had no trunk. It lived in the then swampy lands of northern Africa.

Hyraxes

The closest living relatives of elephants do not look like elephants at all. They belong to two groups of mammals, the sea cows and the hyraxes. Sea cows include the manatees of Florida and the Caribbean, and the dugong, which swims off the coast of Australia. Sea cows look a bit like walruses but without long teeth. The other living elephant relatives—hyraxes—look more like prairie dogs or marmots than anything else. All hyraxes live in Africa. Some species live in rocky areas, and others climb trees.

▲ *Hyraxes are among elephants' closest living relatives. They are rabbit-sized, hooved animals.*

It was another 15 million years before creatures that we might recognize as elephants first evolved. *Phimia* appeared 35 million years ago. This early elephant had a short trunk and tusks coming from both its upper and lower jaws.

One of the later elephant species was *Platybelodon*. This strange-looking creature lived about 20 million years ago in marshy areas. It used its shovel-shaped teeth to dig up vegetation.

Another early elephant was the now-extinct mastodon. Mastodons looked quite similar to the modern Asian elephant and the woolly mammoth, but they were not closely related to them. Mastodons first appeared long before either mammoths or modern elephants evolved.

The famous woolly mammoth was one of a number of large elephants with long, sharply curved tusks. It was covered with a shaggy coat of hair to keep it

▼ *The earliest elephants looked nothing like their modern relatives. As elephants evolved (changed over time), they began to look more like the animals we know today. They developed trunks and tusks.*

Prehistoric elephants in America

Today elephants are found only in Africa and Asia. But once there were members of this majestic group in America. Mammoths and mastodons lived in America until about 10,000 years ago, the mammoths mainly on the plains and mastodons mainly in the forests. They died out because of environmental changes and because people hunted them.

Moenitherium

Phimia

Platybelodon

Mammoth

warm in the frozen lands it inhabited. Our own ancestors hunted woolly mammoths for food until they died out about 10,000 years ago at the end of the Ice Age. Mammoths were more closely related to the present-day Asian elephant than the African elephant is!

Elephant habitats

Elephants live in a variety of habitats. The African savanna elephant lives mainly on the dry open plains and wooded savanna of that continent, although it also inhabits swamps, floodplains, and upland moors. The African forest elephant and Asian elephant are creatures of thick, tropical forests.

◄ *An Asian elephant in rainforest in Sumatra. Most Asian elephants live in a habitat like this.*

Elephants are surprisingly tough. In Africa they exist in scorching desert and near the chilly peaks of mountains as high as 15,000 ft (4,572m). It seems that all they need to survive are adequate amounts of food and water.

In the fairly recent past African elephants roamed across the whole continent south of the Sahara Desert. They followed ancient paths in search of food and water. Asian elephants ranged

Overeaters

Elephants once roamed freely across much of Africa. Now many of them live in national parks. These areas can get overcrowded. The elephants start to eat themselves out of house and home. If the elephants eat everything, they may starve to death. The only way to stop this from happening is to kill some of the elephants in a cull. Culls are unpopular, but they are vital for the survival of some national parks.

▲ A herd of elephants crossing the Namib Desert in Namibia, southern Africa.

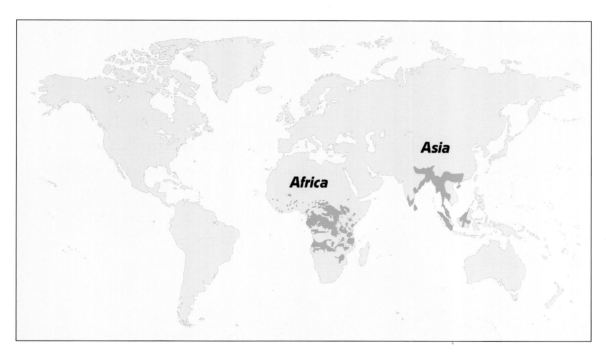

Asia

Africa

◄ This map shows the areas where elephants live in Africa and in Asia.

from the Middle East to Borneo and north into China. Clearing the land to grow crops and build houses (habitat destruction) and overhunting have reduced the ranges of both species in the wild, but they are still fairly widespread. The African elephant continues to live in 35 of Africa's 42 countries. In Asia east of Pakistan the Asian elephant lives in parts of every country apart from Korea, Japan, and the Philippines.

Shrinking homelands

The main threat to elephants in the wild, particularly African forest elephants and Asian elephants, is habitat destruction. For centuries elephants have been losing their habitat to people. As the human population has grown, so has the demand for farmland. Today in countries such as India and China there are few wild places left, and elephants are finding it harder and harder to survive.

Elephants and people

Elephants have had a close association with people for thousands of years. The Asian elephant in particular has a long history with humans. Throughout India and southeast Asia elephants have been and still are used in ceremonies and as beasts of burden. The Indian Hindu religion even has an elephant-headed god called Ganesh.

Elephants are intelligent animals and can be trained to do all sorts of things. In the past huge numbers of Asian elephants were used in the logging industry. Despite the development of bulldozers and other machinery, thousands of elephants are still used today. The elephant's combination of great strength and nimble feet make it ideal for this heavy work.

The African elephant is almost unknown as a domestic animal, and many people believe that it cannot be tamed.

▲ Asian elephants are put to work hauling logs in the logging industry. These elephants are being trained at a government centre in Thailand.

◄ These painted and decorated elephants are part of a festival in Rajasthan, northern India.

India

Of all the countries in the world, India has the closest ties to elephants. Elephants are everywhere. They are painted and ridden in processions and festivals. They carry tourists through national parks. They roam wild in forests. According to the Hindu religion, elephants even live in the heavens. Ganesh, the elephant-headed god of learning and success, is the most popular god of more than 800 million Indian Hindu people.

The African elephant probably is more difficult to manage than the Asian species, but history shows that it can be done. Records show that as long ago as 217 B.C. African forest elephants were being used as beasts of war. Even earlier the famous Carthaginian leader Hannibal used African elephants to cross the mountains of the Alps in Europe.

In the western world today elephants are seen mostly in zoos and circuses. Keeping elephants properly requires lots of space, which is something that most zoos and circuses do not have. But with caring keepers and a variety of things to do, elephants can have relatively happy lives in captivity.

Further reading

The African Elephant
by Ellen Weiss (Wahman Publishing Co, 1996).

African Elephants
by Roland Smith and Gary Ellis (Early Bird Nature Books, 1995).

The African Elephant: Twilight in Eden
edited by Roger Disilvestro (National Audubon Society, 1991).

African Elephants: Giants of the Land
by Dorothy Hinshaw Patent and Oria Douglas-Hamilton (Holiday House, 1991).

The Asian Elephant: Ecology and Management
by R. Sukumar and M. S. Swaminathan (Cambridge University Press, 1993).

Elephants
by Claire Robinson (Heinemann, 1997).

Elephant: Habitats, Life Cycles, Food Chains, Threats
by Will Travers (Raintree/Steck-Vaughn, 1999).

The Fate of the Elephant
by Douglas Chadwick (Sierra Club Books, 1994).

Meet the Elephant!
by Keith Faulkner and Robert Morton (Inchworm, 1996).

Operation Elephant: Earth's Endangered Creatures
by Jill Bailey and John Green (Raintree/ Steck-Vaughn, 1991).

Web sites

www. elephant.elehost.com
www.elephant.se
www.elephants.com
www.panda.org
www.pbs.org

Glossary

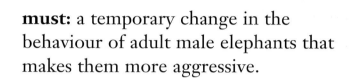

bull elephant: an adult male elephant.

clan: a temporary grouping of several herds of related female elephants.

cull: controlled killing of elephants in areas where their numbers have outstripped the local food supply.

herd: a group of elephants. Most permanent herds are made up of related females and their young, but males sometimes form their own herds.

incisor: a chisel-edged tooth.

infrasound: noises that are too low-pitched for humans to hear but that can be produced and detected by elephants.

mammal: a kind of animal that is warm-blooded and has a backbone. Most are covered with fur. Females have glands that produce milk to feed their young.

matriarch: the oldest and largest female; the leader of the herd.

molar: a large tooth used for grinding.

must: a temporary change in the behaviour of adult male elephants that makes them more aggressive.

superherd: a collection of many elephants from several herds that meet where the food supply is very good. A superherd contains both male and female elephants.

testosterone: male hormone responsible for a bull elephant's must.

trumpeting: the loud noise made by elephants.

trunk: a combination of an elephant's nose and upper lip. It is used to pick up food, suck up water, and to smell.

tusk: two giant incisor teeth used for digging, pulling, and fighting. Elephants are still hunted for their valuable ivory tusks, although the practice is illegal.

Index